Written by

MASSIN

Our whole world revolves around numbers. Numbers circle around clock faces and dance across computer screens. They march single-file through calendars, up and down thermometers, and along a ruler's edge. They hop from page to page, shout from stadium scoreboards, and smile from your door when you come home after school.

Today, as we look back through history and around the world, we will discover many different ways to count and measure and have fun with numbers. Let's wake Pippo, find his best friend Phil (he's the one wearing the pointed hat), and start off on a new adventure—an exciting journey through the world of numbers!

Illustrated by

LES CHATS PELÉS

CREATIVE EDITIONS
HARCOURT BRACE & COMPANY

FROM THE VERY BEGINNING, people counted with the most natural and portable calculator of all: their ten fingers. That is why the most common counting system is based on ten. If we count on all of our fingers, we have one set of ten and then we start over again. Ten sets of ten make 100, and ten sets of 100 make 1,000, and so on. The Aztecs of Mexico and the Mayans of the Yucatan, however, used to count by twenty. Why? Because since they walked barefoot, they could easily add with their toes as well as their fingers. To write the numbers down, they drew pictures of objects that were common in their everyday lives. The number 20 was represented by a flag, the number 400 (or 20 x 20) by a feather, the number 8,000 (400 x 20) by a pouch, and so on.

ON THE OTHER side of the world, the ancient Egyptians—who counted by tens, as we do today—drew pictures to represent numbers, too. A vertical line meant 1, two lines meant 2, and so on. For 10 they drew a pitcher; for 100, a rolled-up rope; for 1,000, a lotus stem; and for 100,000, a tadpole. For 1,000,000, they drew a man with his arms flung up, as if expressing astonishment at such a large number.

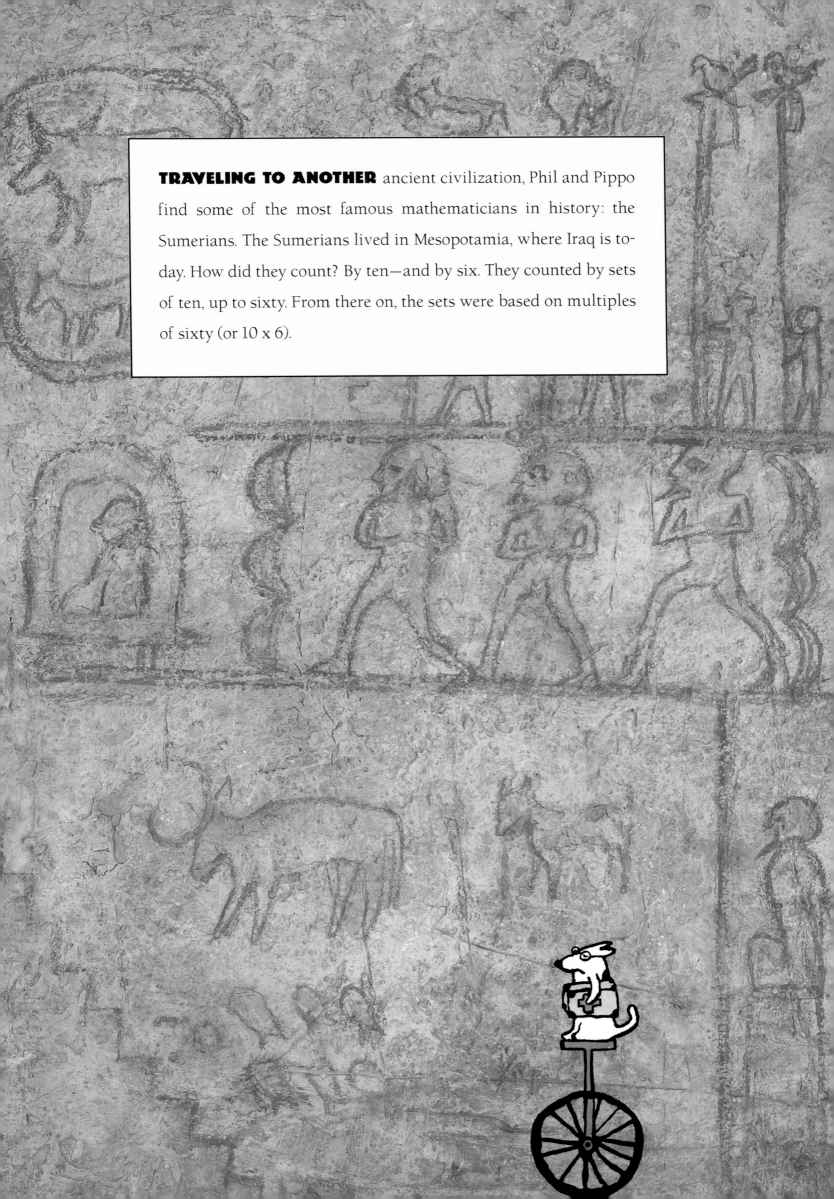

TRAVELING TO ANOTHER ancient civilization, Phil and Pippo find some of the most famous mathematicians in history: the Sumerians. The Sumerians lived in Mesopotamia, where Iraq is today. How did they count? By ten—and by six. They counted by sets of ten, up to sixty. From there on, the sets were based on multiples of sixty (or 10 x 6).

THE SUMERIANS' WAY of counting may seem a little complicated. Yet without even knowing it, you use this system yourself.
For instance, we count minutes and seconds in sets of sixty. When
we reach sixty seconds, we start a new minute, and when we reach
sixty minutes, we start a new hour. So whenever you tell time, you
are actually counting as the Sumerians did!

OF COURSE, there are lots of things to measure and divide besides days and hours. Today, in many parts of the world, distance, volume, weight, and area are measured in the metric system, which was developed in France more than two centuries ago. In the metric system, everything is counted by tens. For instance, ten millimeters make one centimeter, and 100 centimeters make a meter. Counting everything in tens makes multiplying and dividing much easier.

However, Phil and Pippo are finding out that other systems of counting and measuring still exist all around us. In the United States, for example, people usually measure length using inches, feet, yards, and miles. The U.S. system began in ancient Rome, where a foot equaled the average length of a man's foot. For measuring smaller lengths, the foot was divided into twelve inches. In the twelfth century, King Henry I of England decreed that three feet—

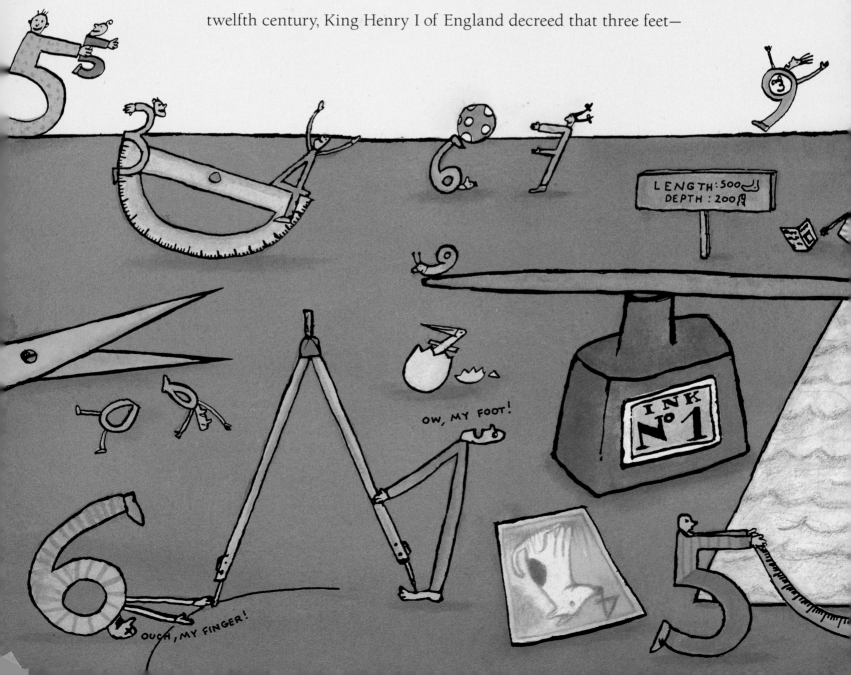

LENGTH: 500 رل
DEPTH: 200 ؏

INK Nº 1

OW, MY FOOT!

OUCH, MY FINGER!

the distance from the tip of his nose to the end of his outstretched arm—made a yard. In the United States today, 1,760 yards (5,280 feet) make a mile—on land, that is. The nautical mile (6,076 feet) is used to measure distance over water.

ALTHOUGH number systems may vary according to time or place, certain numbers may have special importance to many people. For instance, around 45 B.C., Julius Caesar of the Roman Empire decreed that there are 365 days in a year. This was based on astronomical observations and formed the foundation for the Gregorian calendar

that many of us use today. Surprisingly, the number 365 was also important to the Mayans of Mexico. Between the eleventh and fifteenth centuries, they built a temple pyramid to honor the god Kukulcán—and there are 365 steps to the top of the pyramid.

EVEN A NUMBER AS BIG AS 365 could easily be represented in ancient number systems. But what happens when there's no number at all, nothing to measure? Using zeros might seem obvious today, but for a long time, only the Indians and Chinese used them. People in the rest of the world counted without any zeros at all; they simply left an empty space to keep track of missing units. Then, in the seventh century, when the Arabs conquered India, they adopted the use of zero from the Indians. As the Arabs spread into Europe over the next several centuries, they introduced the concept of zero to the people there. And around 1,000 A.D., Pope Sylvester II, a mathematician and scientist, helped promote the use of zero throughout Europe.

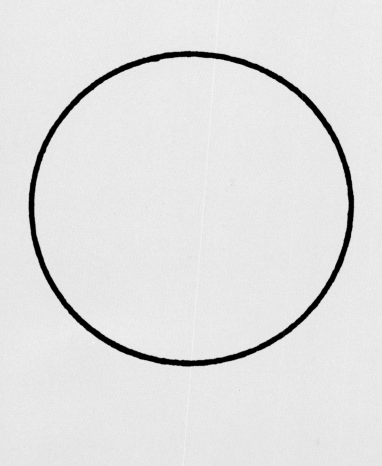

USING ZEROS wasn't the only idea the Arabs brought from India. They also adopted the Indian system of ten digits—0, 1, 2, 3, 4, 5, 6, 7, 8, and 9—which could be used to write any number at all. These "Arabic" numerals gradually replaced the "Roman" numerals that had been used all over the ancient Roman Empire. Roman numerals are symbolized by letters of the alphabet. In this system, I equals 1; V equals 5; X equals 10; L equals 50; C equals 100; and M equals

1,000. Though less common than Arabic numerals, Roman numerals are still used today to represent things like centuries, kings, or chapters of a book. You can also see Roman numerals on clock faces or buildings.

NOTICE
IN ARAB, SIFR
MEANS ZERO

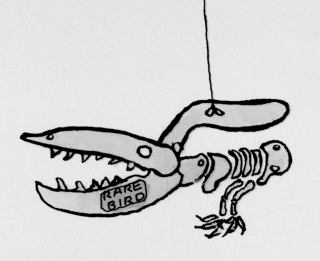

BY NOW, we've seen many different systems of counting and measuring. But are there different ways to solve number problems? The answer is yes. For centuries, people have been able to perform very complex calculations without using digits. They used pebbles, grains, or broken sticks laid out in a certain manner, or they made marks on tree bark. Certain peoples even managed to count to one million on their ten fingers. Others counted on an abacus, or counting frame. With this tool, the Greek mathematician Archimedes claimed he could count all the grains of sand that made up the universe. In South America and the Pacific Islands, knotted strings of different lengths and colors served as a similar instrument.

DURING THE LAST FIFTY YEARS, people have developed another tool—the electronic calculator—to help them perform complicated number problems. Calculators can be as tiny as a wristwatch or as big as a typewriter. Maybe you've noticed that the numbers on the screen of a calculator look different from numbers written by hand. These numbers are called digital numbers, and they are made

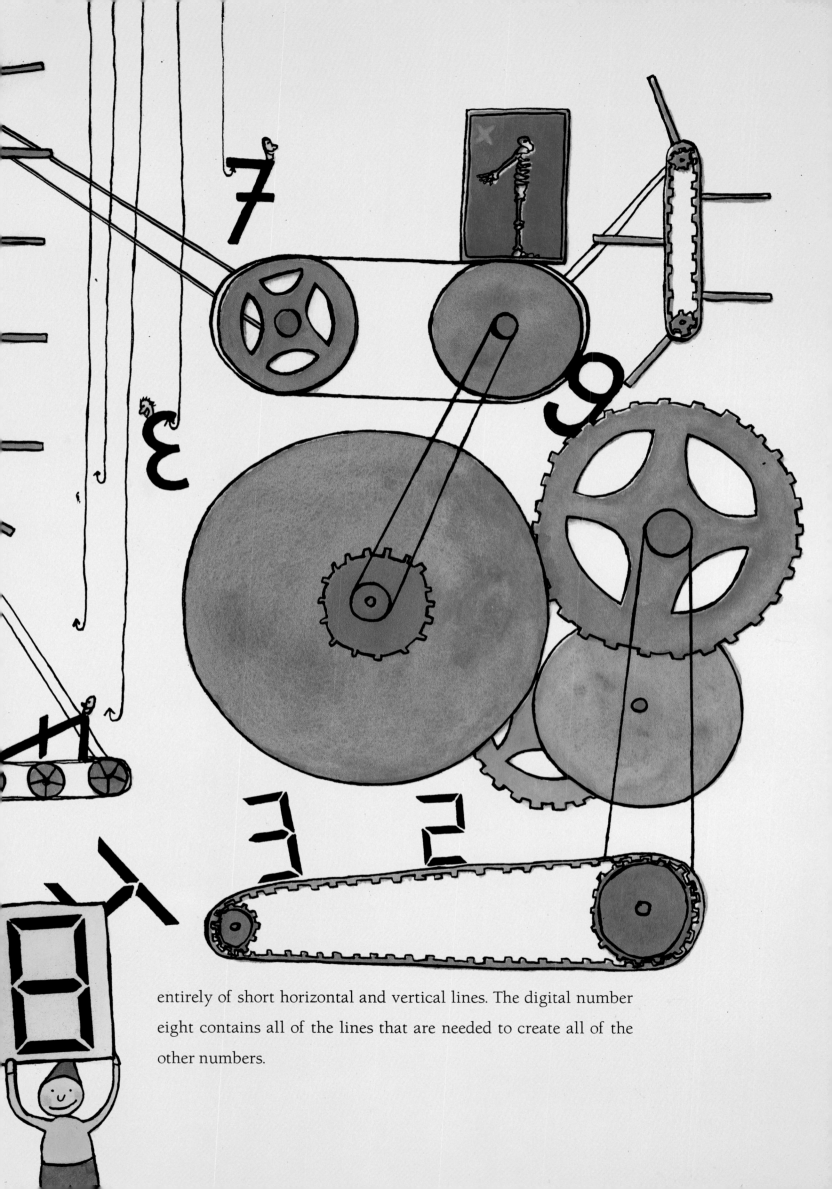

entirely of short horizontal and vertical lines. The digital number eight contains all of the lines that are needed to create all of the other numbers.

FROM FINGERS to sticks to calculators, from tiny drawings of lotus stems to pyramids that sweep the sky, the world of numbers is a fascinating, often surprising place to explore. It is a world that is always changing, even as history itself slowly moves forward.

AND NOW Phil and Pippo have made another discovery: that doodling with numbers can be lots of fun! You can make numbers look like people or animals or just about anything you want. Go ahead - now it's your turn to have fun with numbers!

Text and illustrations © 1993 by Editions du Seuil
English translation copyright © 1995 by The Creative Company
All rights reserved. No part of this publication may be reproduced
or transmitted in any form or by any means, electronic or mechanical,
including photocopy, recording, or any information storage
and retrieval system, without permission in writing from the publisher.
Requests for permission to make copies of any part of the work should be mailed to:
Permissions Department, Harcourt Brace & Company, 6277 Sea Harbor Drive, Orlando, Florida 32887-6777.
First U.S. edition 1995 by Creative Editions / Harcourt Brace & Company
Translation by Carol Volk.
First published in 1993 in France by Editions du Seuil.
Creative Editions is an imprint of The Creative Company, 123 South Broad Street, Mankato, Minnesota 56001.
This is a translation of *Jouons avec les chiffres*.
Library of Congress Cataloging in Publication Data
Massin. {Jouons avec les chiffres. English}
Fun with Numbers / Massin. "Creative Editions."
ISBN 0-15-200962-0
1. Numeration, Juvenile literature. 2. Numerals, Juvenile literature.
{1. Counting. 2. Numerals.} I. Title.
QA141.3.M3513 1995   513-dc20   94-6668
Printed in Belgium   A B C D E
Cover design by Rita Marshall